< More or Less Than > 1-100

Also by M T C Cronin

Zoetrope – we see us moving
the world beyond the fig
Everything Holy
Mischief-Birds
Talking to Neruda's Questions
Bestseller
My Lover's Back ~ 79 Love Poems
The Confetti Stone and other poems
beautiful, unfinished – PARABLE/SONG/CANTO/POEM

< More or Less Than >
1-100

M T C CRONIN

Shearsman Books
Exeter

First published in the United Kingdom in 2004 by
Shearsman Books Ltd
58 Velwell Road
Exeter EX4 4LD

http://www.shearsman.com/

ISBN 0-907562-47-7

Copyright © M.T.C. Cronin, 2004.
The right of M.T.C. Cronin to be identified as the author of this work has been asserted by her in accordance with the Copyrights, Designs and Patents Act of 1988. All rights reserved. No part of this publication may be reproduced, stored in a retrieval system, transmitted in any form or by any means, electronic, mechanical, photocopying, recording or otherwise, without the prior permission of the publisher.

Front cover illustration *Wheel of Fortune 2001* by Megan Keating, copyright © Megan Keating, 2004. Photograph by Simon Cuthbert. Image courtesy of Gowlangsford Gallery.

Rear cover photograph of the author by Jeanette Cronin.

Acknowledgements

Some extracts from this work have previously appeared in the following magazines: *Big Bridge* (USA), *Shearsman*. The author thanks the editors for their support.

The author would also like to thank the Literature Board of the Australia Council for a New Work Grant which was of great assistance during the writing of this book.

*to the apricot tree, the astonishing arch
and other 'wandering landmarks'*

(with thanks to I.C. and C.V.)

1

not simply the stream but they who thought of following

2

and not just running water – how concerned, sometimes,
a group of people with the movements of the clouds

3

'follow me' means three, the speaker
a page of water and they, addressed, wavering,
as the third beckons as well as it can, hidden

4

not just, along the way, vines finding light and its myth,
as myth, invisible, unplants one life for another,
but the unrecognizable fruit they will test with their teeth
for the answer to the tongue's question

5

the tongue, the tongue, steps backwards into a web
respun daily by an appetite that thinks never of holiness
the tongue makes them miniature and blind
the tongue caresses and ruins their splendour
in its own land it speaks the language of stones

6

helped by the small swallow the stone is lifted
from what is crushed and lifted to emptiness, its futurity,
lifted with its earthquake to the place where it is learning
to speak, to the roof of the mouth, that cave of fullness
which can feel the emptiness with which it is filled
covered with breath covered with breath

7

this was their magnifying glass, and not just glass,
but the metaphors, what they see what they see through,
what they see through what they see, one
of the Amaryllis, the face, and the petal is like
a tear dropping down, when fences come down
it is no longer possible to pass from one side to another
incarnate labouring longing the reason won't suffice

8

it isn't simply the difference between action and rest –
there is solace in the sky's reflection and words
will serve any purpose their meaning can divine –
but following to the place where things and words
leave disappearance lonely and smooth as a brow
that is finished for the night with dreams and the place
where they rest is nothing like daybreak –
all is invisible in this morning that has forgotten the night

9

they clamber forward thinking about the concept of forgiveness,
the heart forgives, and not only that but the highest fruit in the tree
hanging like a spindle-shaped shell in an ocean of sky, the heart leaps,
and high excitement about what you can see through a magnifying
glass if only it was not covered with breath, the heart sees though love
is blind, and then the storm of hair over the pillow and the ship
as it approaches the rocks, the heart breaks, think, pure, refusing,
burning, and ache in love, the longest eclipse of the self, and the heart
described in writing always makes the heart look gaunt,

10

literally
the real heart
how surprised they are if is said
something that is not written down
and not simply the kiss but the lips
not simply the tapping but the door
not simply the wind but whispering perpetually through the trees
not simply the stone but the stone
a face, a wall, smooth, rough, always broken
these gentle cleaving feet of the spider

11

not just the spider with its web – one like this
but different, one unlike this but the same –
but the ant rumbling a smaller ground – one small
bit of waiting over, a lifetime – before or after
the event, neither what has been or what is
to come evident in that small word, event,
but a new world spun there, not mistaken,
but still, think, simply of another, and not just
the ant but the cosmos – the enormous miniature
of the universe shaking bones in its palm – not just
bowel, brain and chest but, think, planets and heroes

12

auxesis
was it just that?
glows in hyperbole
impalpable, refusing, loud
meting out life to the body
was it the mud of the mind
creeping with starfish
the tracks they left like galaxies
spinning into sleep?
was it linoleum battering itself
to a small pattern against their legs?
word for word, *agape*

13

they heard the door close
and went to find a place that was away
from them, not only the only place
but somewhere the books
would not stack and the ceiling corners
would not hold and the drip of the tap
would not greet the fly trapped on
the window's sill overlooking the land
where they'd planted the corn, ungainly
tall and destined to dry like chalk
on their lips because of some secret the soil
had not told them, nor the correct
season that would keep their tribe intact

14

they go as far as they can
with the idea of many
not just smiles, gifts, books, betrayal
not stopping at weddings, funerals and the curious
allowance of the celebration of each one's birth
but public dancing, speeches, world
communication and war
what a manied one!
those who pause along the way to gaze
out their windows see the sun overlook
their gardens, see a single human cell
that would find fault with the body as a whole
grow bigger than its destroyers,
than the scream fleeing torture

15

bigger than the big hand with the long fingers of the puppeteer
bigger than the tree across their path
bigger than waiting which, if properly begun, cannot be ended
bigger than the world seen from inside another
than the needle's love
than all they could cram into their hearts
the pros and cons of love
versions of hate
the heat from each other's eyelashes
their grandmothers' graves
the letter-openers
the failed characters from all their stories
the successful characters remembered and carried around
like suitcases
so big, they would not bend, they would make themselves!

16

into three-dimensional models of the sounds they make
when attempting a difficult task
into the inside story of should
into an animal appearing suddenly and becoming an island
into a billowing day
into a scar, the terrace of many flowers
into the true bakers
into the company of death
into the blank noise as they fall of the dreambeats
of their hearts, soft and compact as dark brown sugar spooned
to the heart of a white bowl
into the prophets of angels
into buckets of god
into the numbers which might be similar in song to the bloodstream
which sings like a gold clock holding the unimaginable hand
of time

17

memories flush into dreams in order to stop searching for events
and not just this
they woke one morning to find themselves living in a caravan
on a bald face
there was a petition and more,
freight
sick of writing letters to magazines and the newspapers
they excavated a crystal and moved into
a new house
their first guest was a psychic who assured them of mountains
and the space they claim between themselves
and the flat line of clouds reflecting light
....
they remembered the clouds
(in their dreams)
awake, they asked, where are all the frames gone?
content falling around as if it was torn form

18

their rivals cut down a small wild cherry tree
and they could find no shade
a girl with a bow and arrow slaughtered a deer
and dismembered it in the middle of their harvested cells
from its heart grew imitation and they awoke screaming
'what about the body?'
this was not an accident
the others had been following the movements of the clouds
and not simply the clouds but time listening to thought
and the path of the fish which had never been named
and then, at the point when they knew that the wind
goes back to the sky and mobility to god, they left them
for their rivals then believed in a place beyond empathy
where at the heart of difference they could see
their own face
the heart is in the right place, they said,
in the mouth, in the boots
blow by blow, nothing will ever be stopped

19

they forgot all this and went on their way
as travellers do, as livers do
there was not a moment they didn't fill
with more or less of their desires
the pianists among them gave recitals that tasted of sulphur and geodes
their soldiers slit stomachs and stepped back to allow the unborn
somewhere to fall
the doctors said 'I've done two thousand of these so far this year'
and continued carefully their mathematics
their astrologers tried to revamp situations
that were out of all earthly control
and children grew like fruit
dangling from hardy twigs
they forgot dying
but not by salvaging the moment for being
they forgot it
against their better judgement
they forgot to forget
themselves

20

how early to forget
but forgive them for they must keep replacing themselves
they must keep finding their memory
beneath the magnifying glass they pass
from dead generation to living
yet, how early to forget
the small boat of the nose
the trees' fingers solving puzzles in the sky
the only day of the year on which it is possible
to grow older
the sun, just the sun
ice, just ice
even, how is it possible, the pain in the woman's hips
and her memory which is everlasting?
and the first apricot, the first bread
the last beast of any great size, the last orchid
their children come out and one by one point out
their injuries, without remaining, without comment
and the grown are apprehensive,
but without apprehension

21

dumbfounded with milk
tooth, by the bone, to obtain pure
with heads down they scoundrel the curd
no longer leave anything for the vultures
which have, in any event, vanished
beyond the rock face, are eternally
beyond it
in the sun, the white road and white tree
no tracks, washes and leaves
moon begging them to move the clouds
no sight, a new oblivion
starvation sugared by numbers
they watch, turning away, as lives die
in company, flesh trembled
like a breaking pool
the ingredients are fought
keep their heads down, shorten
their noses, collect their mouths, master
their eyes, shelve their ears
fish rise to their gloves and voluntarily cease
breathing, there is a breakdown in variety

22

the stars of the market
face value
a tax of loving memory
elsewhere compared to elsewhere
M or V or L
a naivety that can be illustrated
by a verdict
what was it they did with their faces?
what they didn't do?
was it the public
in the shops?
lining up
considering the pressures
of the cabin roller case
the proud moment figurine
sledding time or the absolute form handle
suggest suggest reading
the whereabouts of the wreck
and what of legal cutting?
it is as if they search for a reconstruction
jobworths
but what did they come here for?

23

not simply eggs and plums, but knuckles of ginger,
alstroemeria, cold sea salmon, lovers' notebooks,
apples – seven kins of apples, hock, silence,
margarine, margarine, margarine, margarine,
nature, money, the smell, tan, white, private, spray
paint, fish, secrets, fish sweet, burial, gold dust
tastes, cats carved from wood, ivory, bone,
electronic gates, grass skirts, stem cells, calla
lilies in buckets, holograms, the morgue burning
bush cool and green storm flowers, products,
combinations of star dust, star dust, star dust
not simply the memory of a child, but 'a river
overshadowed by cliffs of mud where birds
seem to go insane', eggs scavenged from
the poor, harvested as if from waiting fields,
wheat, their gods, liberated, their gods, maize
they call it, what do they call the ringing of the bells,
eternal, bare-shouldered passing, like the crying
where sometimes people die, carwreck movie,
eviction, what doesn't exist, execution, what
overflows, what sells, people ask all sorts
of questions: does a certain amount of betrayal
mean love does not exist?

24

they sieved love
to find the solid bits
some people, for what they said
were reasons of this or that,
they confined – behind a fence,
in a word, over a barrel
they gave them numbers to play with
they said, play with this number
as if it were your life
and those who tried to live the numbers
fought each other for sanity
and were killed for sanity
and those who counted the numbers
and found they didn't measure up
took needles and thread
and sewed up the holes
between themselves and the new world
the solid bits of love, meanwhile,
were examined for brightness,
for sacred marks, for their ability
to sing in unheard-of languages
that would attract anonymous backers
it sounded like something breaking away
(a glacier down a mountain)

25

there is ice, but no water
their imagination frozen solid
in a life that didn't belong to them
flowers on stalks, but no leaves
strangely marionette and deathly
they felt offended, repulsed
fascinated like children with blood
blood, but only death's veins
moths flying out from anything they touched
leaving only moth-webs and not only that
but everyone in court, everyone in prison, counting
everyone in hovels, moths, or boxes, or exposed
on cemented, bricked, desolate land, moths
everyone in cages, even those on tropical
islands, even those in fantasies, even those
in palaces, mansions, counting, comfortable one-, two-
three-bedroom houses, houses, houses
bookkeeping, stocks, counting, guarantees, fortunes, cries
the little moths' cries, the little cries
counting the little cries
'the crocodile has no heart, no heart,
the crocodile has no heart'
where did their games come from?
not from the children, though only
the children knew how to play them

26

the needle slips into the womb like the eye
of god through the museums of time that
will not go away; have nowhere to go
and so slip down the thinnest metal cylinder
and almost, not quite, into the baby's hand
what is waiting? the consent? the understanding?
the going backwards? they be kind to each
other; they be cruel to each other; sometimes
the same of them, both, in different rooms on
different days; they play, thinking forwards, but
around; they take things from the stores
and factories; they return things to stores and
factories; they see birds and the distance is
peace; they hear machines; they hear the fuzz
that is between the brain and what they hear;
they see a cloud in the sky and it is shaped like
their country; they all come from different
countries; they have pain anywhere; in the
amniotic fluid they have a home, rime,
antennaeless, a huge antenna and the absence
of time passes like a breeze on a holiday, eating
from banana leaves, from bad news, their
nursing of each other, lifting, carrying, cleaning,
wiping in the face of paralysis, no speech, in
the absence of personality, what they know,
their ignorance of the iceplan, the sunplan

27

packaging stones
skies of badly burnt bird
sirens that left catastrophes
and became real
are packaging stones
and not simply stones, but thresholds
of days
they record laughter
to play to the child when born
did the needle pierce it?
spellbound the child is born
actually in silence
as it is a moment no scream pierces
tell me of the ant, says the child once born
and the stone puts forward its hypothesis
and the child is twice born
and thrice
as the child, the book, the sand
as the flesh, the question
the word, the answer
what flows and passes and is unborn
birds chase each other in circles
the table is emptied
and the mother's rest collected
to become love
they share the shadow
the shadow of the cliff, the tunnel

28

they ask why they must always travel
even paralyzed they must travel
they are certain there is an answer
and so continue passing through
tall grasses, the ends of the earth, the earth itself
fields of daffodils, desire
they eat meat and know famine
from books they return, again and again
to the body and are unconsoled
they sit beneath trees
and take firm hold of the fruit
from end to end of the fields
drop their crutches
wonderful!
their pale enthusiasm, washed over and over
by the light that has the whole
afternoon to range over
is vital
they hang their teeth around their necks
and silent, live in the moment
what if tomorrow they are questioning again?
what of it?
beasts come to watch them
at last there are beasts to watch!
and the grasses whisper
and the trees shake
and the ant, the ant breaks its gaze
from the rock in its path and listens to their hands

29

on their day not simply tears
but shoulders for them to fall on
not simply scarves
but unworthy mouths for them to conceal
not just the crime but the one who committed it,
witnessed it, judged it and passed sentence
and not only fortune but the corner where
fortune breaks and sobs
and god?
that is the instinct after the instinct
has been boiled and stretched and seared
once it doesn't know itself
and goes looking for itself
how beloved to know
how impossible to be possible
if it finds a hand, it says to behold is god
if a mouth, it says the word is god
if a foot, the way is god
this is how their shadow was thrown
both ways
and they found themselves pursued by memory
unnarrating grief and hope
with death following, not waiting ahead
all they heard they related to error
the water singing its last/next place
but the song being composed
for the next
the futures then they began to intuit
are what must be unlearned

30

reality runs hidden alongside them
the pain-point for eternity
with the photo-monster
they try to pierce its pleura of love
with their cotton bibles and rainy tongues
they introduce its representation
to the throat
with full bellies they try
to live the side of them that starves
they think about their ancestors all the time
while their country hobbles
on its charred black leg
they dig in it
looking for the day, the light, the syllable
that is larger inside than all their languages
they plant the acanthus and the laura
they plant the god-seed which never sprouts
but from which they harvest beads
they discover that a child's finger
can cover a mountain
they discover the audience of themselves
the peacock brutality of desire
they learn how to assume
causes and forces
they discover facts
eventually they remove their eyes
for the sake of death and its furtherance
and then hear the voice of the clay
their eyes will see forever
its sound is like purpose that has no care for itself

31

scream-shot
all the names are in between
the name that is never written on the grave
(it waits for justice)
the grappling names
those corresponding with the gamut
hearing the universe begin
they write in ash
the lines of two alphabets
so that the lines cross
annihilating the sign and sound
of what is central to speech
this is the teleology of enation
ostentation
the *faute de mieux*
a bundle of rods
the possibility of ending up
forshadowing all likelihood
they act as if they were the crocodile
languishing on the ocean bed
and slowing its heart to three beats a minute
waiting two years between meals
but never feel themselves drown
never notice the ache in their bellies
satisfied at last by simple time
their past words knock
on the roof of the ocean
but they hear only the small breaking suns
of their dawn chromosomes
the mercy scratches of thread-like fibres
scrabbling to birth their sense of self

32

not simply the day-born, but what they allowed
to come from darkness
pieces broken from their bright souls
the spectrum dying into white
not simply what was seen only by the eyes of the night animals
but the restoration of dust
the settled to that moment when it unsettles
the unsettled to where it rests
they called for what was owed
(this caused their world to break into parts)
they demanded that the mornings
follow one after another
(this enslaved them in a timely ambition)
they wanted to see how all creatures died
(this was a curiosity that resulted only in excuses
which held their own tails in their mouths
like the leashes which bind answers to their questions)
they invented heroism
but no-one remains a hero in their own lifetime
and they found themselves in the bodies of birds
fed poison from rooftops and city squares
they found themselves in the chisel
that would not carve the name of integrity
on the waiting tomb
they were in the slur of the stroke-sagged tongue
in the invisible blow that submerges the ribs
in a fear of breath
and they tried, in their most prominent places,
in their places most hidden,
to remember the words, to retrieve the words
that might have been spoken in chaos
but the words flew, dead and fast like stones

33

the dead man had a great voice
it faded away like no other
resoundingly it died in their ears
like a tired animal in a tunnel
with its own ears taken between
its fluttering paws
in this act it left them to their imaginings
which contained no trace of the voice
not its water
nor the stones hidden in its sleep
not its green rib
nor the masses in its soul
and though the existence problems
have been solved by countless little voices
before them
voices that took mystery from its analysis
and cradled it
still they seek, with science, with expenditure,
with murder, to find solutions over
they have questions perpetually changing
and think them new pinnacles from which
to call 'Plam! Plam! Plam!'
they seek to bring their own days
out of their mouths
the crushed anxieties of desire
emptiness with its nooks and crannies
a road of stones with the land riding above it
on the quiet word of faith
each brick of that wall speaking
a portion of its silence
they wheel from their mouths trolleys
bearing living bodies with curved knuckles
and fallen eyes

34

they ask with these the last questions near death
they want new new (all the time)
they don't listen (all the time)
to what's already known (all the time)
even monkeys can do this
fuck for 8 hours straight and lose 50 pounds
they finite
they fuck the life era
they insert reasons with disabilities
into their flesh
all the time all the time
are they looking at shadows?
have their mothers gone to look at shadows?
who is looking at the shadows?
they promise forgetfulness
set their ship adrift among inactive flowers
they are de facto (all the time)
cutting a path (all the time)
navigating the one-way path (all the time)
paradoxa, acceleration, the 40 x 40 x 40 plan
their wings are a token
their wings are in place of a voice
that records its own sound in the story
they are beyond reports of its strophe
marked out by fabulist hooves
there is the prism of it turning
swimming light perpetually and colour
the carousel
rock-crystal, rock-dove, the heart, a fish
of light
the news is over
they believe in disaster
now all that is left
is how they say it

35

dog, they said
they said the fact is echoing
the one who fought
has stopped to mark souls
with the fingerprints
of joy
what's in that mind?
in its custody?
all that was said
not so much
what was used to decorate
to solve
they said too too too
and there were some
in lands where a single word
could not
……………………..
its tongue taken immediately
to the box
lid lift-
ing and in
with the other tongues
so here, all, they said
and all was no thing
and there, today
is the day and the world
ended –
and rolled back
towards them
worse than never to be heard
than patience
than the kingdom
or the other one
they said, think
it's not about

36

forever
or the olive trees they planted back this way
from there
ten triangles on the top of a ridge
ten ranging from purple to black
the occasional green or scarlet
why is there a white line around everything?
is it snow?
is it light?
emptiness showing through from the emptiness
behind things?
is it the halo of the cry
that is cried from all things?
horizontal, then vertical, falling,
rising – a mountain with its peak
suddenly tipped bedward
over a river, a sea, an ocean?
a hand in a flood propping its bag
upon the higher ground it can itself
not reach?
it's not about survival then
they learn from their hands
but the way life adheres to the slopes
as it goes and then ceases as if
each point on the way
was a summit, as if
each summit was a valley falling
between other lives, those
that go on between the trees
forging their shadows to populate the house of night
satisfying the ants of that house
with the crumbs
of their eagerness
counselling the wolves by its door
with what is truly haunting –

to live

37

a dish with a room in it
they fill the dish with contradictions
and not just what was not
its own fulfilment but the myth facts
the burning circumstances straight from the pit
as they sleep off all
questions
someone said 'those who find it unendurable
should leave' but the promise was in
the walls and not being
set adrift –
nothing was adequate to what should be
renounced and none knew the number
one
a well was brought up
from underground and examined for its loss
of vision and in the loud, confused
sound that followed the earth
was found to be sun-
proof, a place where the war
starts suddenly and no longer any
correspondence for a
star
like the broken moons that scraped
around those short and cold and
noisy nights and made
them noisy, it lived
inside a
cave
they would catch a stone
or a bit of wood, the next corpse on their
right they dragged home for what was
split, the two futures, the eye and what
takes advantage of the
dark, the little rush and the

challenge – they were each alone, they created
the minute they touched

38

grammar
earth-smoke
thorax
feast
preservation
virgin
diving-birds
feed
event
notch
magnet
fence
defied
blank
prophets
season
cadmium
interior
firmament
comment
title
wit
relinquishment
ewer
wiolin
nihilism
artefacts
newlyweds
perfect
prancing
theatre
moon-vine
rice
plotting
wanton

medicine
mystery
cretonne

39

not simply a cloth, a purse, a blind release
but a green between nature and more
the existence of painting that surpassed
all their ideas of motion and a stillness
stern as any prow, as any accident
intimate or flawed, later or routine,
as a hand in the small or another together
like couples do with no acknowledgement
between them; not simply also music
on the unusual spread of limbs to avoid
using rooms but a circulating summer, a
pearl chance, a learning, elegant plate with
a lap for the century to lie on, a woven
cord, a key, a chord with its centre
absent for the face to crawl in to express,
sing, and not just these: signs, signs in cotton,
signs in dye, signs in ink, signs burnt in,
the right way up, upsidedown, signs sideways,
angled, effaced, scraped, scratched, etched,
completed, incomplete; the spot, the stand,
the mark, of the thing, and the mark not of
the thing, a trace like some thing cleaned
and another a trail, signed or unsigned,
desire uncoupled from the hands and left to
flutter with curtains, a free language, a
language freed from the line of them and
residing in the street, flowers overhanging
their representation and actuality, real flowers,
stealing bruises, what they want with the
mouth, not leaving it in the after-word but
always taking it forward, not simply the
baton but the message, the new gist burned
to the hand with pain's alchemy, another line
for their eyes, nerves, finger to follow, follow
and not just follow but the forge, the guess

that cracked within, the path that made itself
a path, the go-back, lustre, unabridged time
that held them ripe for the toss and favoured
verbs, verbs, verbs, a bit, a bit left over

40

air from the fan
opened the field
and in the open field they saw
death drop down
and roll in the warm sand
its eye contained
the dreams they missed
when waking to the old cock
of betrayal they poised
for the world had arrived again
they all recognized it
stared at its new face
they had never seen before
and genuflected
what would they do with birth?
sacrifice it to life?
define its time?
subjugate its source so the tearing
that continues always can be dulled,
ignored?
death at first they feared
then went to with a bowl of fresh water
then entertained with pattern
and richness
then engaged in games about names
spoken and unspoken
then turned their backs upon
death at last they feared
and then banished
to a position beyond their ever-widening
kingdom of knowledge
sadly overlooking (sic)
the obstacle now in the minds'
path – barrier, circle
and line –

to keep death
at bay
what an unnatural majesty –
when the fence comes down
they are no longer on a side

41

in what shall their rest reside?
do they ever leave their clothes carelessly
upon the beach or in the woods?
do they listen to their restlessness?
is a series of steps, a journey to them,
do their lips tug at the air
as if the air was tough meat?
unlucked, will they weep in that place
where they wait for learning to begin
and when fate doesn't turn to beckon
will they grasp the time
to move on?
in every bit of ignorance
they were busy
without acknowledging paradox
they took its name and lived
beneath its banner
they saved
       – for personal futures
       – for days when they would
         not be able to move
       – for elation
they made vacancies in their hearts
and put downpayments on catastrophes
because of and despite
they cursed
they cursed on both sides of the hill
they cursed with and without reference
to books
in their towns they talked
and in their countrysides they dreamed
of the end
of the end
and they dreamed of leaving their world
and starting again in the warmth, the new light

and they, continuing
continuing
continuing
what is the proper result?
what is that thing dead
around the edges of their memory?

42

is it the other side of the body
what speaks from what was prevented
as they prevent what they can
and should, and should
leave the rest to fate
as if there was an arena
and not only that but themselves
as both spectators and participants
the outer and inner circles
giving religion to each other
as alone they have no religion
no agreement like that of shapes
with a mind that comes upon it
and assembles it into such agreement
truly scattered like ice-floes broken
and adrift on the moor of the sea
but skipped from and to by legs
balanced by hands led by head
and lured – yes! lured
it might be the strangeness of a horizon
why the mountain appears as a line
how everything in the distance becomes the same
might be gratitude
might be peace between everything
might be desperation untethered
and to approach might mean
to move ever-further away
away where the ice won't support the foot
where the face blurs in passing
where it is easy to die because the cold
is kind and pre-dates god
and the stories of god
and everything is blue and white
or looking closer, black
and the movement beneath the mother's hand

is attributed to the mother
and never to what might appear
until it appears
and even then remains and becomes both
what it has remained and what it has
become
nothing of what was walked – just a step

43

the whole point
the whole point
the whole point
is to head somewhere?
is to go somewhere?
is to get somewhere?
the curse of between
not being able to *be* the end they see
not being able ever to begin as they have begun
they had ceilings of plaster pressed
into every imaginable pattern and design
they had patents
amazing adaptability
a massive desire to kill and own new coats
they pretended that shadows
were only found in corners
their laboratories received and gave out information
that was of some use and not of some use
everything was said to be of the greatest importance
as it lost its importance
people swapped blood
and organs and tissue
people sometimes exchanged body parts
with animals
men went by with the leg of a pig
with the neck of an owl
they wore sunglasses
they wore incoming information strapped to their heads
and spewed words out as if that
would make someone hear
things were ready-made
as if the situation had no need to arise
bins came with instructions
so they would know their rubbish without needing to know it
birds came with instructions

poisons, ditto, so they could poison themselves
no risk, just expense
no risk of finding the true pleasures
which had been removed from the shelves
and stored at the wrong temperature
for survival
no risk of survival
or of needing to know it

44

they knew it was the last hour of their lives
and knowing this became tired
and having lived all their lives
slept
in their sleep was a red light
a notch
a dress
a fence
some sand
and a waterfall
there was a son
and a cow
and a daughter
and the forest of agony
she would give birth to
they waited in that forest
to know themselves
in the way they were
in another way
but found only snatched things
things that didn't fit
biographies
broken pools
cloth that wouldn't fold
rope that mimicked bones
worlds made purely of judgement
worlds already made
already made
so what was there to do
and it was this way they made each other
already made
and while they made each other
unmade the world they dreamed
abating, unfilterable
it was of the nature of heredity

perfectly-remembered
imperfectly executed
its supersufficiency making them frantic
its potentiality stripping their actions
back to wakefulness
where they were obligated, required
adjudicated and determined
it is here they were forced to see
life's relevance to death

45

life unravelling
how it arrives at truth
not the same thing as what is true
they can't work at it
every skeleton has fifteen bodies – more!
every body has thirteen mouths – they could be eaten
all at once!
they not only become dizzy trying to think about
their countries
they watch as people
become small inside
they pay money to hear their own voices,
the voices of those they love
they stand in public feeding money into the inanimate
breathing the voice into what might be coveted
they disdain
they are seduced
they disdain
there are things they could quite easily be aware of
they think the dead are lost
they think they can find the dead
they do not look for the time they are wasting
they do not know that this time is accumulating on a plate
that is offered to them
when asked about it they say it runs out
they have become very sensitive to pain
they are very aware of pain
they ignore pain
they let their arms hang down and not only this
they have forgotten the true meaning of the hand
what do their lungs do?
they do not know
nor anymore how to possess what occurs
what other way is there?
why do they not ask?

their prayers and requests all have to do
with an excess of desire
everything becomes beautiful, all heroic
as they reduce their world to understanding
as they understand the cosmos
as they understand god
they countenance evolution to here
but not from this point
they do not believe how what they know
kills depth

46

and what motive did they have?
for measurement?
for comparison?
for what fits?
ultimately, they would not stand for death
they refused to agree with themselves
with the ways their bodies sought blindness
and deafness
and to exhaust the touch
they wanted to believe they were born
and again and again
that they were not fleeing at night
from the night
that it was not gravity
that gave their skin its softness
which they fought and fought to save
they gave their judges hundreds of pages
of explanations
of reasons
for why they refused
to carry their gaps around with them
they wanted to travel light
laden only with accessories
and unpleasant weapons
they characterized themselves
as people against all odds
their language soon contained so many words
of justification
that it was always easy to speak
not simply possible
for example, they referred constantly
to their houses as homes
when the doors they opened
were onto cupboards
they spoke of great desires

revolving around reflections
and images of themselves
never realizing they resembled a total eclipse of the moon
which unlike that of the sun is not dangerous
and can be watched with the naked eye
they even started to talk about time
as if there was more of it
where that came from
as if there was some unspoken co-operation
between their understanding
and what it might be of...

47

for example
they claimed to understand planets
how opals grow
when in fact what they knew
was the art of cutting and polishing
and the sorts of things that might happen
sand would forever elude them
and libraries become full
with the paper clot
of their denial
they court-martialed a man
who opened a window in an air-conditioned building
and against all odds
kept writing poems
they starved
and chewed on dried pigs' ears
and fed their dogs dried pigs' ears
and skated on frozen ponds
and rockhole by rockhole searched
for poisonous crabs to milk for biological warfare
and tiled their bathrooms in neat rows
and manufactured expensive brushes
for their teeth
and appraised art
and sat in the dirt waiting
for the screaming men with swords
they became excited at the birth of the new novel
and balanced their best words on technology
and a standard of living
they became emotional in tourist offices
and stood in throngs inured to death
and another death
they wailed
singing in their sleep
betrothal, genuine complaints, burying food

for a day their government said
was future-proofed
again and again they pushed out of stomachs
and stood up
and developed appetites
they were reflected in a drop of water
they looked through garbage
they travelled through time
they were shame-trained
and forgotten
and grossly underfunded
and walking from their shelter they looked always first to the sky…

48

the idea of a man walked past them
brushed against
that part of the mind
where the image hardens
they begin as studies
a hand between the breasts
and another pointing downward to the groin
the eyes look suspicious
they are sitting surprised
there is a dark shadow to the body
and in the ocean, symbols
in the green verge, symbols
in the redly built cities
in the flesh margins, symbols
the things loved, cherished, idolized
are things not like them
they are things that do not live in time
flowers, music, children
and so studies
they are dead
study them
compassion for them
dreams of possession
from their terrible stage
they appear resigned to their false elevation
they glide
they double
through evenings
the days
they concern a woman
they concern a man
walk with them
with their motionless listening
they accuse of forgetting
of panic

of creation
they are exiled by every act
they are the juvenile
the mysterious private god who walks
in the dark to learn how to walk
in the dark with the help
of little modelled hands
little modelled eyes
the roughishness of walls
unnoticed desire
they stay with their poetries
ambiguous, motherish, they raise their voice
to name their children, ambitiously, the months

49

they talk
how they talk!
a thousand poems of light
adorned with the seeds
that inhabited the olives – Ur-becoming –
mind-chaos
the sound of who
they get out
they get back in
themselves
discriminate
they know chairs
they know emptiness
even night with its local moon
banishing legends
what's written in the stars
the recipe
for a man and a woman
but dust
and sleep
the grey of an egret
long-legged on a slope
a tree
imprisoned
expanding into the house
at the end
of the eye
where they sleep
sleep is whole
the body
at the only time
it does not live
for compensation
or privacy
and they sleep

stretched out in their own hands
soft and unyearning
in their own murmurs
the shape
of flight
as it unfolds
as their feet
toss
and what shifts
shifts
(imagination, said a great sage, is not sight)
sand
the wind
they weep

50

their souls have taken them
their children are immortal
death remains
life remains
one giving birth to the other
being all to each other
both in their moment of coming into being
smaller than the pinpoint
smaller than any metaphor could make them
they have spent all their time
trying to find life, trying to find death
in themselves, outside themselves
they found genes, they found DNA
they found protozoa, they found prions
they realized the sun was killing them
they worshipped the sun
and then they didn't worship the sun
and the sun kept them alive
there were some who hoped
even though they couldn't feel it in their gut
but they couldn't deny it
they believed faces
they developed names for other faces
they discovered how to become huge
and not only that, how to reduce themselves
to the essential murmur
to the love that fades in the ear of the sleeping
lover, to the dream that privatizes itself
as the dreamer wakes to the tyranny
of one who wakes from dreams
they made themselves new
with genetic information
with the oil of flowers
with the knowledge of their future pain
their children's pain

there was no time in which what they did
that was good outweighed
what they did that was bad
they spoke and then didn't speak
they created languages and then ground them
to ash, to earth
they fed and then burned each other
they called their lives a journey and then
pretended they were unaccompanied
they did not see who was always turning
to greet them
the word they had put in their own place and
finally, when they had forgotten the present
they solved death, immortal,
they developed the art of accident

51

I, my I
it is ruin language
you fall into me
and are born to what?
this extraordinary justice
we shall be to each other
as alone we could take no part
I call you my door
my table, my nest of ants
you are yellow, you are every colour
there is your black, there is your hip
I peel the world away from you
and expose your invisibility
your disappearance
your no need for its wealth, its poverty
interminably I open you
I open and open
you shiver and disappear
my eyes, like other eyes if they had ever existed
focus on what fades
this is love
to want what dies
leaves before the broom and the body
growing into the size of the head
shrinking again to what might enter
all things, everything
the ash of flowers
mixed with the ash of you
wood's ash mixed with the ash
of you
I plan to drink your death
if I can steal it from the day
think, think, how to make the new me
that is not the same as the old me
ending dreaming

lick the roots
gamble how far
the heart of alterity is nourished towards death
behind the infant lurks the journey of death
death runs back to claim us
from the point at which forwards
greets its own illusion
are there words which can stand
in the place of belief
that is, where it is not known
what to believe? *you*
you are always simply what I might make
you are myself replied
I cannot approach you
I can only approach

52

I talk along
as if on wheels
what they call chatter
mute conversation
avoiding chaos
in its chaos
but my mind is postponed
chance noise choice
sleep slams in on me
indiscriminate
leaf dark sound of green
inadvertent moon
night to stop things
more or less than
what I don't know
others' chairs
empty of the object
are not chairs
soiled feet
soil the bed
aquatic! that's what sleep is
bubbles of talk
curtains
a grey card that drifts by
eternally on the tracks
as the tracks
are eternal
as is
the expansion of the skull
the proclivity to damage
oneself
to get the body
beneath the nails
and lever
and rake it

to measure it up to
the unreal parts of oneself
even trees have that life
the imagined part
the keeping part
that is always losing
quivering
like a dog's nose at a locked gate
like a man's hand on the blade
that would cut the sphere
into infinite slices
I imagine these shapes in my head
wonder when it was that the birds stopped staying clear
of my shuffling feet

53

I kick them out of my way
such soft bodies –
helpless against me
now that I am unrecognized in a wilderness of heart
music that falls down thought
what is talked about
at the well
what is lowered
what is drawn
you watch from your room
this performance of summoning
from way back in your terrible death
where the room is still
an agreement of shapes
around you
you watch and do not know me
with my heaviness
balancing wanting and waiting
on the two beauties
of my shoulders
I remember your hands on them
in a dream
when I stole your body
from its true dimension
and conquered what had unbecome
in me
the lack
the deception
the tools of largeness
thrown
at your feet
there was no goad
no lash
no fire or jolt
no spirit

but a single voice
the flow of our throats
like two lost rivers
into a torso
no distinguishment
no adjectives
to go with anything
it seems I must wait for your death
for the realization of you
a door opening
against my legs
dimly your face
the end of January

54

we pass things back and forth
between us
ends and beginnings
sterile bottles
the scribbled on scraps
from when you still thought of messages
to leave
sand caught in my clothes
and brought indoors like bird-flocks
snow, reminders
of an appointment not taken up…
you sang in your sleep once
and I wanted to feel your lips
but was dreaming too much
of all I wanted from you
it's too bad really
how often it came to that
my greed
how often I thought you were shy
when you were really
unconscious
do you remember, I'd ask
strolling from garden
to garden
never waiting for your reply
which always came
from a world hidden in the body
you would be betrayed, you said
by what you felt
and would die from what
you would never feel
you never screamed
though I heard you cry often
from human tissue, you said, thirst
your tongue a nine-long net

in the water
the sky
and yet you never once over-reached
did not suggest outliving yourself
you sorted through the garbage
for the glass palm tree my mother gave you
in the beginning
and made me stop the car so you could throw in a bin
the only book you've ever written
that was (somewhere between here
and a holiday
a million lightyears away)

55

your motives
no longer have a master
you know now
the measure of a smile
how it compares
to your enormous inability
to make it believable
how easily I accept
even a hint
and no longer compare it to the laughter
at all those old jokes
we were once capable of
or is this only the truth
in the time I'll excise
from the time that normally runs
the same time I take
so that I might believe
I am a part of what goes on
life, we say
gravity and touch
reasons to move
taste
but I've given up on judgements
here where language has shifted sideways
into full acknowledgement
where there remain no reasons
to justify or define
no reasons really
for me to make it possible
to put my hand on your hair
nothing is found in what is this real
desire finishes
upon an idea's acceptance
and I understand you are stardust
my fingers will never rub

you are always
at the mercy of the universe
and like a child
who has not yet discovered his heart
I ask no questions
I bring you quartered oranges
on a tray bearing
a pointsettia uncoupling
from itself
I bring you the images
of a fruit and a flower

56

I take from you a plate
is that the truth of it?
the plate from which you have removed nothing
with time I become more familiar
with your life unravelling
more familiar with the body
that shows through your body
your mouth is closed
now your mouth is always closed
I watch as you become small
as you bleed out and disappear
into everything
I hear your voice though you do not speak
I hear your voice of refusal, of acceptance
try again to seduce you with what
you disdain
all you are aware of
are there parts of you already dead?
shall I find again the action of your body,
your body in a moment without pain?
every day the plate grows heavier
and the outline of you more faint
I feed you your hand, your lungs, words
I might speak
the thoughts I never shared – time's
reluctant seeds
you take only what I do not offer
a future so slight there is no room in it
for my desire
all my prayers and requests slip there
into the wrong tense
you understand nothing
as if I was yet to love you and there was no time
through which you would wait for me
is it true that we are missing

from each other's lives?
your arms possess you
there is no longer anything else to possess
all you will never know, the last depth
the days falling behind
as if they had tired of you
I do not hear your voice
from the silence I cannot retrieve the gods of presence:
your evolution towards me
which will never begin

57

is there an hour?
and if so, where does it start
and where does it finish?
has it been rendered solid?
has it been spoken about in words
that can do to it the justice of light,
of shade, of the play of one thing
with another?
you are sleeping again
how long with your hand under your face
I do not know
you know, sleeping, someone else
is born from you
it is obvious
someone you do not know and who knows you
intimately
it is a birth with no pain
a birth purely for the other
it has the meaning of new
you though, you sleep
with your legs lost in the forest
how still they are
how completely lacking movement, lost
everything from here is lost
I've already lost the cupboard filled
with your clothes
I went looking for it this morning
and found only a pool of quicksand,
a door which kept slamming
and not just your dresses
but the mirrors you looked in,
the basket of fragments,
the curtains pulled aside by your hand –
all gone!
your world is unmaking itself

and leaving me in mine
where all parts
are displaced and nothing rests
in an original position
I have been forced to execute drawings of it
to determine a place for my body
which is also now, unknown
it is as if I am being ordered
into the arid lands of my own unshareable future

58

you said there is no point in somewhere else
especially if it exists
you said it is comprised of a very fuzzy set
during circumstances are other circumstances
there is no need to see
no need to think to resemble
in order to survive
you said my thorax is no longer my thorax
my life no longer pertains to love
and pleasure
you said to me when I was astounded
there is no longer any reason to turn around
you may keep turning your back
and I didn't turn…
you said it's not important
and I didn't turn
I could see the moon
and it made no difference whatsoever
I didn't need
to describe it
I could see what was hidden
you said I sleep now through all their deaths
their estrangements
and the barysphere may as well be
the stratosphere
you said I have my own blood and organs
and tissue and they are all of no use
it is easy
difference now catches me by the throat
it is the same
as it was when you said once upon a time, but no,
that is the wrong story!
and my profile, my vowels, my mysteries
have rejected any pattern or design
which might begin another

you said I can hardly take this seriously
I feel like I might be a pig or an octopus or a
very sleepy little spider
and there are no longer any instructions
I might be tempted to follow
I said I need you
and so I need you not
to be human

59

breath mixed with what cannot be breathed
that is what impressed me today
as around your lips a blue halo
yielded finally to expression
to the ocean's mercury ceiling
my grief is your volunteer
it rises bearing your body to the light
you struggle
you swallow me and try to choke on me
you set a bubble adrift in your brain
but the laws of earth don't apply here
your lips surround what might be the whole of the world
your hair is an assemblage of animals
your hair in favours like a restful volcano
I am a wolf
your fame, counsel, shield
in collaboration with your death
I will take the message of you to death
the song of your passport
the never sign of your broken wings
have you finished everything?
have you no loan, nothing to be lured?
have your feet passed through the earth,
have you no anatomy?
will you leave twice?
will you leave three times?
is it true you have lost the ability to make promises
now that you can forever forget?
no morality
no ability to float
no orders
I have seen that today you have lost interest in the horizon
you no longer bear scars
you no longer trespass, imagine
now you let me go!

my face blurs
and I can no longer see my own face
everyone leaves – the fine, the finite, the fit, the title, the life
vibrate me with your fingers and their calluses
made entirely of music
your hands opening up the wood
deep and deeper

60

what shall I use for people?
where shall I find some eternal substance
like the mind with which to open
the universe again?
what with my feet – steps?
and my mouth, does it lose words into the air
as if the air buried breath?
how might I find the place
of your entrapment and learn its vitality,
its fatedness; do you beckon me
to leave time
and its movement?
I am ignorant of you
and with this I busy myself
I do not recognize your dead body
and yet identify it as yours
I am paradoxed by you
from your pockets I save
      – your possible future
      – my hand, which did not mean
      what I thought
      – 24 hours, then another 24, then another
all then, was reverie
the catastrophe had come, one-legged and balancing
cursing me for remaining beyond
its arms
its relationship
cursing me for being because of
and despite our relationship
and I talked and dreamed
and started up cars and warmed the street
and banged doors and lulled by the sounds
of people waking I drifted towards
a new end…
that's all it takes to drift off, just

us, all left
all caged
and living
is this our result?
in it will there be enough imagination
to create the memory of your death?

61

rain hit the air today and angled
in the field you lay like a compass
I would come across
and know direction
the brick aqueducts let pass a train
and your eye contained, suddenly,
the movement of lives passing
the waking of faces to the outside
of the world
what does not contain them and lives
only to be recognized in dreams
I stare at your new face
your face seen ever before
and pray
I have now seen your birth
how you sacrificed yourself from death
and entered time
how you tore your body from another
and continued with a born body to tear,
to be torn
you said, yes, fear
you said, yes, water, I know that
for what it is
you said I will not respond
to the demands of my time
and my place
I will turn my back on the smallest denial
I will take fear
and blood myself with it
I will listen to the voices that speaking
have spoken, that speak
that they have yet to open
their mouths to speak
I will see knowledge stop at the wall
and waver and declare its ground

I will keep it at bay
my majesty will be
focussed on the waiting
on the haunting that is waiting
waiting for colour, for the slum

62

have you ever stood before a painting and
not just the painting but the moment in which
it does its verb to you, stood in I, in-clothed, in
covering, in purse, and been done, a tree in a storm,
a roof, a drainpipe, a sun in a storm, a palm with
lines growing along it, a weighing machine, a break-
ing crippling still that was a sky, a trajectory,
a series of hearts of varying colours and strengths,
a why not a why, the wrong kind of non-fiction,
the story pivoting itself on a button, what was
lost, what was going to be lost, what you would be
losing with your select ideas, signs non-signs, contagion,
type, words not written by hand, stripping then revealing
humanity, the body buried in your unreadable
script, your fingers my body, the softness of the lip
before the club of the tongue, the several imaginable
seconds, their heaviness taking my breath, lover's eyes,
the mind's another way, and would we, would we meet
somewhere with our wings laid aside, with our spaces
snatched, our giant rock feet halfway down the para-
graph of our hearts, sleep pinched to the menial office
of our survival, what community in our little book
of questioning, never closed in all the time we slept,
hands undone undone by what we search into,
unwhispered the hortative language galloping on
the shelf between rope and tether, flowers over-
hanging the judgement which would take our
names to where we had no passion for them and I
call you me and you call me me, our names are a
poem, looking at the past is a poem, born, hark,
ourselves, not others, their shape and the fragments
crushing in the palm which holds tomorrow's eggs,
thinking light enters, night dark enters, the same
curiosity enters, disappearing the verb, it arose with-
in it but I don't know what it is, bitter enters, sweet,

I had no right to say you wouldn't die, *how hard was it to remove yourself from this line*, but I have made it my right, make strings your strange theoric heart, the ship on top of the water, pointsettia

63

vernacular
cave
pleura
hour
intimacy
breast
battle-cravings
need
whistle
prey
excavation
seduce
price
wishes
terrifieds
passing
titian
vista
ballot
donation
biography
fit
prophecy
coir
stereo
indeterminancy
urn
delight
soundking
puzzle
moon-trees
oblivion
boiled
persistent
broken

caramel
unblushing
jute

64

above the ocean
I bring you a dish filled with the dry
low groan of thunder – let blackness dam
its share of the room and leave us
a corner in which to reveal the beginning
of invisibility, the inside
of the mouth
have you seen the grins on the faces
of the saviours after you turn them
away?
we never had what they had
trust and learn and trust yourself
in this emptiness where shrine-
less we offer each other the allegations
of our telepathic
dream – someone has to play god!
I hear your eyelids opening
as if I had forced all the situations in which
I was capable of suffering under
your pillow and commenced
to foretell all the memories of our
pity: *we are all wrong*
        no-one, no people, is not wrong
        in those moments
        when we are not wrong
        let's consider our past
        and future wrongs
but my mind is a stone mind and puts
a stone on my chest
this heaviness too
is for you when just turning
that way it happens from the crown
of the head
it is sadness that makes you
invisible, realization

coming only with the beginning
of invisibility

65

it is not about survival then
but your last act, your most recent
act
you look away in that moment
from past words,
tastes
constancy becomes a finely spinning
spike that holds you and anchors
the posthumous history
of your breast to your
living breast
is it snow, is it light
pouring like ash into your face,
or is it all you left
unfinished when it became obvious
you would abandon your
life after courageously futile attempts
to finish it?
'I've never been to the back boundary'
you said but I watched the veined
light and dizziness that trailed
like lovers behind
your eyes
we are what illuminates death
by saying it
and the world has ended
for us all
yet still we trip over exposed
roots and mark our days by memories
of falling fruit as if any
small end would pretend
our life and prepare us for the vigil
to come
why though, didn't the wolf tell us
it is not sad

to be dead?

66

dog puddle
an empty soldier
licked the light
of smiles departing
the dead
shutter-crates
offering in the hurt-space
we prosecuted them
from what we had in mind
rugs, treatment, a concern
for talking
so much was said
that it had to be said and said
but what speech values so highly
is silence
the hinge
like that once word
that killed every man
dividing up your
pineal gland
and so the day
is the day
you said
specifically they want my mind,
but utterly?
they do not want
my mind
but my senses, mixing
that person
over there
will you phrase me
other than this language
my lover-in-the-war
think me
about it

67

why did you think of an arrow?
because I didn't think of anything else
we are all the same
we are all the same
we are not magical
we are not strong
we think we are magical
we think we are strong
why are you poor?
because someone broke my house down
we make the love-sound
with magic we cut a path straight to the heart
dipped in the rosebowl life comes out all red
we are never READY
tanner of the skin of desire
the scar is a terrace of many flowers
no longer beating this heart,
this last neverness is like a friend
navigating a path
for which we are never ready
but blind upon it
we are full of desire
full of desire
our students are in the unknown stripe
that runs alongside us
have they told you the news about your body?
your body you gave me?
have they told you?
the dying have the mountains
we spend our lives making
they see the names vary
they hear the stripped phrase
how deep?
only to your own depth

68

I heard you hearing it
my heart which contains
all the variations of your name
like the belief that birds
in the season of migration
hibernate at the bottom of ponds
and lay a vast egg
from which hatches ignorance
and the eyes-closed myths of knowledge
bordered by yielding
by ten soft hands
which seek the mouth – the out-
infinity seeking the in
I would spend all my life in your mouth
with its sad light
blue light of the moth
there I know the brides of the wall
have polished the floor
with their tears
the sisters of the corpse
draw over and over
(as if making one, arrival and departure)
your vatican head
there I would study for a degree in architecture
I would perfect my life as an adjective
I would pass a legless woman
pushing her baby in a carriage
I would steal the direction of your tongue
while taking the shadow
of a thing between your teeth
you chew a line between yourself
and the sun
ineliminable light habitating your eyes

69

quiet bright day
day with the hole at its centre
laying the chaos on the table
the black hat and its wearer,
invisibled
did you think there was no fear here?
I feel like I have never been alive
but I am!
pave my tongue with readies
get on a nut and look at my tree!
look at what has turned up again
after all my fathers!
a face!
curse-lost, fury-bled, nevered!
the blows of my movement
throw life out to the side
the selections I make from what is discarded
remember the words
and like air that has taken help
make a voice
like a little balloon which screams
'don't lose any of the words'
and that is when I tell you
what I have been thinking about you
through a crowd of dust
your south
your pity
the lonely, lonely sun
that accepts only what it has destroyed
and because of the caged snakes of my eyes
your mouth speaking like a sling-shot
just barely filled with present tense

70

flay the names
unface me
the head-shell locking the butchery
your butchery from mine
the coincidence of our eyes
what we admit
– 'love ideas'
– reporting on the bias
– the accountability of suspicion
the paper I am writing for mass consumption
involves you, me *and* the experiment
the child that was bombed
out of its mother's arms
on my windows are reflected horror,
a fountain of blood,
the need rose
with its thorns that you did not feel
this is all in accordance with how it is
right from the pit
where we mean something to ourselves
where your smile reveals a narrative
chased by death to exhaustion
where you exhibit no discomfort
when I crawl into your chest
to find what expression your heart bore
when confronted
it had the look of a face pissing all over the floor –
nice and tight and autobiographical
with that hint of resolution that comes
with letting go…
and I knew I would go unrecognized

71

and because of love, all omens spoke of love:
body – the body's death;
our pleasure – sadness
I heard my heart appear
the harp and blood-ash falling
our own, our own
our own tears, our own shores
washing into the sea
our own black line
between the earth and the sky
our own dark torture
the clay where we shall put our eyes
the company of our eyes
self-encouraged
to sight death and death's thought
no eyes, just this noise
the rumbling that never ceases
the sound becomes the killer of a god
and even the trees bent before it
all matter engaged
in the monstrous conversation of form
art-song, land-grave
nomos birds seeking the high-memory
unwhispered
in the fair side of your face
my desire for you so less conventional now
that your desirability is taken away
all is unsustainable
the tail of the comet
ends at my mouth

72

we have no instinct for each other
every inclination
is one which contemplates us
shadow has no love of light
over and over the light is broken
by this ignorance
the sun in the tree of the day
is seven suns
and seven suns is the star
we close our eyes on such a star
we tell each other our other names
these are the names which know hate
the children of the feather
the ones that sink the ink
through blood and bone
they are the nocent
perching in to me
they are the statues and their words
scripting the play about the preparation
for a new holocaust
one outside the ongoing holocaust
what is split
living
or at least as we perform the terror of it
we are all unrequited,
not someone else
you live my life
as if the soil had taken me, alive
how am I to live?

73

I can only live in moments
periodically you do your whole life at once
at times I wish you would stop dying
I am partial to dreaming
and prone to sending you messages in code
I have certainty
I have gathered up the grass growing at the world's end
I have gathered up the buttercups
yellow size and alive
I have passing desire
which petrifies my love and feeds me my own heart
as if it were the meats of the owl
the rhinoceros or the horse
I know about possibility and famine
but should love be inconsolable?
whenever you die near me
love takes up more space at the ends of my hands
they search my body for the scar that will form
when we understand beauty
do we?
that things are not as they should be
is why I watch
why I wait for the passionfruit flower
that fresh-blood colour that even ants
can see is travel
but the grass is whispering ant-things to my heart
and my heart is dead
should the trees keep shaking words upwards?

74

by this time the stone is the stone in my hand
water it knows as well as wind
crushed grasses and the smoothness of glass for an instant
and also internally with uncountable memories, souvenirs of scale
colossus discontinuous, now fractured belonging to every grain of sand
and then in the end-polish to every haunting grain of sand in time
this is the musing aspect of stone, wind music in the long bones
'thinking about' roughness, the smooth nuance in the creek bed
but what about a table when you turn it on its end?
the cliff?
what of the tunnel?
did we wish to go through it even before it was there?
air and water and fire seem to shrug at us their ambiguous shoulders
and we are breathed or drenched or ignited with some conventional
desire which abates as the element abates
not so stone!
stone has presumed us and any convenience is its own, it says
'you can never feel me as much as I feel you
but flesh, when it thinks, is greater than all which destroys it
can be saved even by its ability to pass thoughts beyond the death
that is life
but something so firm, that does not slip through the mind and body
like water, fire, air, life or death, is beyond potential
though not temptation
look at your statues, bridges, roads! so definite! so terminal!
you see your end in me, the end you make
and so whatever begins there eternally escapes you'

75

we go backwards, have you noticed that?
all the time, you are more prepared to be a
child; what kind of moment passes that
allows trust to thicken like that newsworthy
water that turned to wine and then to blood?
we grow and lose, have you noticed that?
you arrive and leave over and over and I count
that you are arriving and leaving, calendaring
my days by ideas of growth aligned with the
microscopic thoughts of seasons ranging from
the fresh firm shoot through the preparedness
to bend of the mightiest branch on the final
tree with a leaf to acknowledge us in the last
green hour of autumn, an autumn of the mind
in which we find ourselves unkind to our
children and sitting in the cool blowing afternoons
unable to move from the view of this window
onto the cradle and this looking-away that is
the way we live since we have found our
shields and our fame and counselled ourselves
with pride fearful like the stories of misfortune
and the dead; they have recalled us, our dead,
and we have recollected their way of life as we
breathe under the buildings while the earth
moves as we move while the earth breathes; I
can't hear you breathe; what are you, my love?

76

the no last number
I cannot count
the moth I want you to be of me
the cage I am never in
the laboratory, the present
I cannot go to
the game, the game
you are playing over there
with the children of puppets
while I spend twenty thousand years
growing up
shine, ring, vibrate
your betrayal winks at me
like an angry and frightened horse
on alternate days
you call me crocodile
heartless you bounce and shine
put a fantasy on the steps of our home
grow tentacles and strings
and demand that I move you
through our motions
you are the cliché that imprisons
me in my blood
you shout from a box
that the phone is never ringing

77

the phone, and footsteps
the phone
footsteps
the phone
the phone the phone
and footsteps
it sounds
like something breaking away
footsteps
count
the rings the steps
the needles between the toes
the solid bits
breaking away
it sounds
like that
the phone
and your footsteps
their brightness
their bits of love
their sacred marks
it sings
like a new language
you cannot answer

78

no, betrayal is not the key
the test of love is love
....
....
....
....
....
....
....
....
....
....
....
....
....
....
....
....
....
....
....
no more, our god, just that

79

we had an intimacy made out of things
we valued momentarily
and now the closeness we have is created
from materials of comparatively little value
will the meaning of this
be discovered in the discrepancy?
what can be learned from the fact
that we are moving towards what *we*
define as worthless?
I resisted becoming you (my fear was not redemptive)
your words were a waxed thread
I slipped along
your dictionary of punishments
served the purpose of exactitude
wherever I opened it my uniqueness was harmed
and my capability astonished and confused
with perception
my hands reached beyond our home
and picked rocks to throw back at our roof
I did not want to live with the unassailable
but tried hardest to save those who did
what I would never have done

80

I brought you milk filled with another woman's spirit
yet still you drank it, you said
it made you lay eggs, you said
it made you sleep on a mountain, beautiful
cold grappling with influence finally falling
cradle out of my custody
so I brought you bone, as if
bone had passion, as if
I could be present to you like hunger
or a bodily function
waves or allowance or the exponential
trapping we did of each other's future
actions, except for the days
I brought you suns, roads, trees, moons
which you remembered perfectly as life
and threw at me as if they had only been
a frame of mind
aesthetics didn't help, nor did my fingers
beneath your chin moss grew over everything, you refused
to lift your head finally
I started war, morality

81

remembering everything
the dilation of your eyes when the bomb hit the roof
the sun, just the sun, falling
flies in the strawberries
everyday life made so extraordinary
that we came out of the bunker and simply ceased worrying
how part of your face, sectioned away,
was more beautiful than your face when whole
ice melting over the bruise that covered
your belly and chest
ice, justice
how we talked often about why there wasn't
a shortage of water
were there no animals left to drink it?
were there so few of us?
I remember that time didn't pass
and so I am still living you
the first bread we stole
the cup, no handle, we drank from both sides
our children, growing huge with apprehension

82

a way to lose myself away from death
a way to be dying so that I cannot feel the dying at all times
more, and not quite that,
a winter-asleep
a spring-wins
an ongoing not even ordinariness
but just what might be enough to keep the moment
cradled within its own worn hands
the breath clean in its perfect dress of flesh
more, more-or-lessness,
the whole of the body bathed in sun
or what might be like it
this is not cliché but simply simple
the moment *is* warm
not the caught or forced one
not the ungrasped or felt one
but the forgotten one in the forgetting
forgetting is so far from the body, so body
forgetting is so far from death

83

your body needs to find its bones
in the fish, the hull, the breaking wind
too many words will crush the heart
even the word 'pearl' with all
its accretions of beauty can kill
does the shadow learn to speak
from that which casts it
or from that on which it falls?
even the first time I saw it
your face was familiar to mine
and deep in what we share
where no animals live that we do not know
where no plants grow that have names unknown to both of us
is a place strange to you and I when each of us walks alone
I am afraid, you are afraid, of what we are
do you believe in what might lie beyond empathy?
did you know your rivaless has her heart in the right place?
she says go in the opposite direction to where sympathy lies

84

there are shopping centres where everything inside is the same colour
you can buy little bits of it for your suicide personality
white!   the colour the brain sees so perfectly when smashed
against the in-bowl of the skull
I dreamed it, not pure but unsure, fearful
the loud rotten snake of course, the hotchpotch
might enter the dream with rights to repair the wounded mind
with whatever is larger and more kind
usually chaos
we know, when awake, that light radiates from those
who cease to grasp themselves
this light is bodily
solid like the tiny house in the vocal chords
where tone lives
can you hear it? – between clouds, nestling quiet
the skin of the monster
is the skin we touch

85

ear drumming on the back of a mad fly
a pig with a broken spine hurts like eating my own tongue
violet is the landscape's colour
ask a bird
a whole yard full of mulberries calling 'don't look at the grass!'
the other side is where identity stops
the other side of identity is a spot you can jump to
only when the destination is hidden
my daughter is a pig who can't talk properly, or as a pig should
people have been changing themselves
into clouds
into pink flowers without heads
it doesn't bother us that birds are now living in houses
the first exercise is always in perspective
my life so far away from me and very small
it might even be a little hand on the end of a duck's arm

86

what is bigger than the clock embedded in you, your private burden?
on different sides of this room we have missed something
that won't happen for another one thousand years
how is it I know that if we had been in a period of having sex
you would not have been able to resist the full eclipse of the moon?
and this is so though I sit at your desk and write
I am naked
this always makes the heart look gaunt
sitting, naked
all is accelerated, the silver letter-opener
and you ask about eyelashes
what about heat? what about staring into your eyes
and the pros and cons of love?
you always imagine the lover still and the quiet is-it-there beat beats for you
capture it – make yourself larger

87

death started in the joints of my fingers
they would not bend, even to pick up the knife
the windows, like hard bones, kept the day out
and I could hear the voices of the trees, in stone beats,
the diffidence of my only heart
it is only against what is solid that love scrapes
and shapes itself as the lasting wound and scar
I could hear singing in the bright hard dawn
and screaming, perhaps weeping, in the decomposing
seam that joins each night and day to the next
but the rock was calling me into its thick heart
and when I went out the world was empty
it was not only you that wasn't there
there was nothing the same and nothing changing

88

when the season comes, the door opens
shall we find this without the help
of our own hands?
the books fall like a waterfall over the mind
and our ceilings apologize to the stars
for their blindness
this is a quiet house
the sounds within it are like the movement
of a foetus when night has settled
the dripping tap, the buzzing sill,
the screeching cobs of corn against
the sky's dark board, we all crawl inside
the tribe's womb and wait

89

a gape
was it what you tore with your own hands?
your literary voice?
what you spoke made palpable despite softness,
loudness
was it what you refused?
they, from the other side, who we reflect,
say that the god refuses, that god's descendants refuse,
that the ocean refuses, that sleep
refuses the mind unless it creeps
was it the galaxy
spinning like a fired starfish to make us edgy and doubtful?

90

cut the world in half with the knife
inserted right between my feet; open my hand
and find the frozen earth; plant the apple
seeds of my fingertips inside the inner walls
of my chest and, delicate, thin, watch
the new world grow from there, pulsing like
the folded-back lips of a pap-hawk
suckling at the breast of the spider, ant,
bones of the shaking chest of the cosmos;
tell only the truth and grieve only for such
cause as that, think, burning, swearing

91

you kiss and you blow through the trees
far-off from these lips and whistling perpetually,
lightly, in a wind occupying a world absent because infinitely
detectable, rising and falling, above and below your ear
like a stream flowing, purely of light but sounding
like water through tall reeds and sounding like many breezes
dripping through leaves and washing against the curtains
before falling again through a window and leaving you here
with only your mouth, its small breath and locked door
did you notice me standing there in my boots and coat

92

knocking, tapping? think back, you always saw the lover moving
and the thumping heart propelling that and more, if you look
at what you've done I'm sure you'll admit it hasn't transferred
to the page – to be happy you must be faithful to happiness
but you kept changing your shape, any beast would do,
and throwing fruit, shell, rock, did you think I lived for you,
what is your love but this war with reality, borne down upon
by a featureless stone horse, mountainous, blood the slave
of its veins and high-black scream?

93

you sit under a tree with your blood too old
to make anything work, you sit under a tree one day,
one day unusually, and in your chest there's an electrical
fire that's as tight as pain, breath being heaved with the effort
it takes to sink the same bit of earth you've always
lived on, cliff passes by, petals lift up like hips
in desire, only once the sun lifts the clouds onto
a painter's canvas, gold, like a new corpse

94

incarnate labouring longing
I can already hear you telling them,
it's your imagination
one of the writers separates each sentence
and in those spaces
where the darkness is kept dark
I can hear your breath

95

we breathe not for oxygen but to expel the air we have husked
to dirty ghost; we are under the black river where we breathe
despite being land animals; this is how they put things in packets
force them in; when I try to speak it feels like having my face
ripped off; the words float up to the surface; language blossoms
opening; but I can't hear what I'm saying; I'm under the black river

96

what is sour? the body after it has been in the mouth
for the space of a night, the sweet lemon rolled
in your tongue and unfurling like a daffodil?
flicking over and over the fine skin of a coffee bean, sweetness
growing spontaneously in the sacred dwelling of the mouth

97

along the way, not just the dark quotes,
the chipped off light of utterance unmeant and skint,
but all the regions of the tongue drawn by surfaces
the tongue slides: *can I let what I have go – into us?*

98

call me, when you need to barely touch; every
visitor, the taste of a whispered world; every
path is a furrow; find us, the uncomfortable stars

99

and not simply time but the kind of second that passes
only because of words – how concerned with effects…

100

ice follows water follows

www.ingramcontent.com/pod-product-compliance
Lightning Source LLC
Chambersburg PA
CBHW032052150426
43194CB00006B/510